*Ofélia*

# Ofélia
## *A Taste of Brazil*

PRESENTED

Josimar Melo

PHOTOGRAPHY BY

Sergio Pagano

DESIGNED BY

Victor Burton

KÖNEMANN

© 1996 by DBA ® Melhoramentos

**Editor-in-chief:** Alexandre Dórea Ribeiro, Walter Weiszflog
**General coordination:** Maia Mendonça, Adriana Amback
**Executive coordination:** Adriana Amback
**Assistant designer:** Miriam Lerner
**Recipe text:** Adriana Amback, Cecilia Salomão
**Culinary production:** Cecilia Salomão
**Art direction of the photos:** Sergio Pagano
**Photographic production:** Paula Zaroni
**Assistance:** Dempsey Gaspar
**Editing:** Plural Assissoria
**Graphics:** Victor Burton Design, Estúdio DBA
**Lithography:** Mergulhar Serviços Editoriais

Acknowledgements:

Aleotti, Ao Moto Elegante, Arte Nativa Aplicada, Aruña, Casa Nobre, Chinon, Designers, Doroti Riotto, Empório Santa Maria, Estação Saudade, Euroville Anitqüa, Four Winds, Jorge Pessotti, Ladelli, Macau, Sèvres, Stella Ferraz, Taki, Tri Art, Vila Rica Artesanato, Willian & Gilbert

**Original title:** Ofélia, O Sabor do Brasil

© 2000 for this English edition
Könemann Verlagsgesellschaft mbH
Bonner Strasse 126, D – 50968 Cologne

**Translation from Portuguese:** Julie Martin in association with First Edition Translations
**Editing:** Andrew Mikolajski in association with First Edition Translations
**Typesetting:** The Write Idea in association with First Edition Translations
**Project management:** Andrew Davidson for First Edition Translations Ltd., Cambridge
**Project coordination:** Nadja Bremse
**Production:** Ursula Schümer
**Printing and binding:** Stige SpA, Turin

Printed in Italy
ISBN 3-8290-4066-0

10 9 8 7 6 5 4 3 2 1

*To my daughter Beth, my son-in-law*      *António Jorge and my grandchildren Juliana*      *and Rodrigo, with much love*

# Table of contents

### Starters

### Fish

### Meat

# Doces e Docinhos

## Desserts and sweets

# Pães e biscoitos

## Bread and cookies

# Nowadays,

we all take for granted Italian arborio rice, fresh French foie-gras (goose liver pâté), extra-virgin olive oil, cheese imported from the four corners of the earth. The finest ingredients of international cuisine are to be found in countless delicatessens in the major cities of Brazil.

But… what about cassava and pepper sauce? Or bean paste? River flour? "Pequi"fruit? Strange as it may seem, in cities like São Paulo the typical ingredients for regional Brazilian dishes are harder to find than rice noodles imported from Japan. And yet there is no doubt that the culinary excellence found in Brazil depends less on exotic specialities from distant countries than on the assimilation of local Brazilian cooking – extremely flavorsome but ironically almost forgotten among us. For unless we understand the basic elements of our food, which make up our gastronomic heritage, I doubt whether we would get very far in terms of creative cooking, no matter how easy it is to learn the techniques of international haute cuisine. Far be it from me to harbor any chauvinistic prejudices. At the table in particular, how could we possibly regret our access to the production of other countries, especially those guardians of the great art of cooking? There is no question of rejecting the delicacies of other cultures. But we must simply understand that we are part of this great hotpot of flavors – and if we do not appreciate our own heritage ourselves, nobody else will either. It will be lost. Learning to cook the Brazilian way is not something that can be taken for granted. Regional dishes are not found on the table every day from one end of the country to the other. The history of the influences, of the culinary habits, of Brazil is revealed in different ways in each region and in accordance with the many traditions which it is so imperative to preserve.

The most native style of cooking, the most authentically Brazilian, comes from the north: in the Amazon region the ingredients are indigenous to the point of being almost crude – cassava and its derivatives, fish from the river, forest fruits and produce.

In Bahia, in the northeast of Brazil, African ingredients and seasonings lend special aromas and colors to spicy dishes which are unforgettable to anyone who is trying them for the first time.

From Minas Gerais, in the centre of Brazil, comes the assimilation of the Portuguese influence, which has resulted in a cuisine which is rustic yet full of secrets and inventive solutions, from pigeon peas to "tutu", a bean and bacon stew with cassava, to the extraordinary pork crackling.

In the south of the country, Brazil resembles its neighbors with the "churrasco" or barbecue, the trademark of the gauchos on the pampas. In the mid-west river fish graces the tables together with game. In the northeast again peasant cooking combines with seafood.

Publication of a book of Brazilian recipes offers a glimmer of hope for those who fear for the fate of our roots. The strength of the enterprise is reinforced with the signature of Ofélia Ramos Anunciato. Ofélia is a pioneer in popularizing recipes in Brazil. And in the world of broadcasting she is not only a pioneer in Brazil – where her television program has been running for four decades – but also among the foremost, and undoubtedly among the most enduring, in the world. Her success on TV has catapulted Ofélia's books to best-sellers throughout the country. Ofélia has turned her program into a showcase for broadcasting everyday, simple dishes, which mirror the intermingling of so many cultures which typifies Brazil today. For her popularity to be channelled into the dissemination of dishes which form part of Brazilian history, preserved in a style normally reserved for works of a different cast, is pretty remarkable. Bon appétit!

Josimar Melo

# Ofélia Ramos Anunciato
# To all my friends throughout Brazil

This year I shall have completed thirty-nine years in my profession, thirty-nine years of *"Ofélia's wonderful kitchen."* There are so many stories, so many memories! Sometimes, almost involuntarily, I find myself remembering, going back in time…
When did it all start?
Even as a child I was interested in the kitchen. I remember the ranch of my grandmother Maria, in Garça. Every day she woke up really early to give her orders to the gardener. I was very young, about six or seven years old, and I used to walk behind her, quiet as a mouse, hiding behind the cabbage heads. One day, despite all my caution, she spotted me and said, "Why are you following Granny?" And I answered, "Because I want to know what we are going to eat." My

grandmother never forgot that story. With my grandmother Maria I learned to make bread. Every other day she baked bread on the Garça ranch and when the oven cooled down there were scones. There were also home-made cheeses and the fruits from the orchard which were turned into preserves and wonderful desserts. My grandmother used to serve up a steak which became famous in the family. She fried the steaks in a big frying pan and gradually transferred them into another pan beside it. Then in the first pan she made the sauce and put the steaks back one by one. It was absolutely delicious, with lots of onion-rich sauce. I was the only one to learn these secrets, thanks to spending so much time watching my grandmother at the cooker. For a long time my aunts would all ask "Ofélia, make some steaks like Granny's!"

My first experience in the kitchen was also my first prank. I think I was about eight years old. My mother and father went out shopping and I decided to fry three dozen dessert bananas which were lying on the table. I cut the bananas into slices (just imagine, almost seventy!) and fried them in the oil. When my parents got back the kitchen was a cloud of smoke. I got told off but my father thought it would be a waste to throw so many bananas away and made me eat a big plateful.

Time passed and I found myself living in Santos, already married and with one daughter, Beth. I really enjoyed cooking, trying out new dishes with my family. One day I received an invitation to work for the *Tribuna de Santos* newspaper. They wanted a daily column on cooking. I was recommended by my husband's grandfather, who was working there. I accepted it as an honor and had to learn to type very quickly. Not long after that I was asked to make a program for the town's Clube radio station. It was a one-hour magazine program which dealt with women's interests, fashion, beauty and of course cooking. One day Mr. Rebelo Jr., one of the directors of Victor Costa TV, met one of my girlfriends at a party and asked her for an introduction to me. When she asked him the reason, he replied:

"To see if she wants to make a television program."

When my friend told me about this conversation, naturally my response was negative: "No thank you very much, I wouldn't know how to do it."

But Mr. Rebelo wouldn't give up and his greatest ally was my own husband. The very next day I got a message to ring him and my husband returned the call. From the corner of the room I signalled to my husband not to accept the invitation.

"You can take it from me, she'll be there, when is it you want her to come?"

"The day after tomorrow we want to do a test."

That is how my career on television started. It was 1957. The dish chosen for the test was "Tender ham à la California" and that was because Mr. Rebelo had been given two tender hams and didn't know what to do with them. At that time we still didn't have freezers. The test was good, I was calm because I knew there were no viewers. When it was over Mr. Rebelo gave me a piece of advice which I have never forgotten: "You see that red light, that's your public, address yourself to that, that's your friends out there watching."

The day of the first performance arrived, in the Radio Clube auditorium which was full to capacity. I didn't go to the hairdresser or anything. They just put on some powder to

reduce the shadow, because TV was still black and white. Nowadays it's quite different, there's a whole production team to accompany me. The program went on air and I prepared another "Tender ham à la California." I was shaking inside but I concealed it with a calm face just put on for the benefit of the public. When it was over I was showered with bouquets from all sides. I gave a lot of autographs. And the tender ham – well, I didn't manage to take any of it home because everyone wanted to try it. And that is how the program *Ofélia's wonderful kitchen* actually began on Victor Costa TV, every day at one o'clock in the afternoon. After six months I was invited to work for TV Tupi in São Paulo, where I spent ten years. I remember one particularly funny episode from that time: my program was part of the women's magazine presented by Maria Teresa Gregori and it was the day before Christmas Eve. I was up till the small hours shelling chestnuts to stuff a turkey breast. I got everything ready and went in to São Paulo to make the program. When I got there, I had forgotten one of the baskets in Santos and I had only brought the cassava flour, a tiny amount of seasoning and dried fruit. I leant against the wall and felt as if I was slowly fainting. Then I had the idea of cooking the turkey breast in slices, because when it was cooked it would be the same gray color as the chestnuts. Before the program started I asked the cameraman to keep well back and Maria Teresa not to ask any questions. But she was very absent-minded and walked up to me (we usually talked quite a lot) and asked, pointing to the turkey breasts, "What's that?" The producer signaled to her to be quiet and I trod on her foot. She looked at me sideways and I answered "Chestnuts … they're chestnuts. But let's talk about the festivities, have you bought your Christmas presents yet?" Maria Teresa understood and we swiftly changed the subject!

In 1967 I switched channels. *Ofélia's wonderful kitchen* moved to the Bandeirantes network, where I still am. Cooking evolved very rapidly in those years and I am proud of having been part of that change. I have also done twenty-eight videos, countless fairs, cookery courses and gastronomic festivals. There were so many events it's impossible to count them all. Of the more than thirty years with *Ofélia's wonderful kitchen* I have some very special memories, particularly those which involve my friends. One day a woman wrote to me saying that among all the programs on television, mine was her favorite: "I take in laundry, my husband sells popcorn at a high school, the children are just children …" She watched my program on her neighbor's television and was writing to ask me for a pressure cooker. I found her letter so simple,

so sweet! "The children are just children" means that they didn't do anything, they were too small. I sent her the pressure cooker.

There was another incident which also moved me very much. One day I wrote a recipe for coconut ice for a magazine. Some time later I received a letter from a fifteen-year-old girl telling me that she helped her mother to bring up the other five children. Her father had died in an accident and her mother made my coconut ice and cut it up for the children to sell on the ferry to the island of Guarujá. My God! I was crying so hard I couldn't even finish the letter. What a wonderful person, that mother. All her children were studying and getting a training. There are some things you never forget. Unlike a lot of people, one thing that makes me very happy is when people stop me in the street. They come up to me, men or women, and within five minutes we're talking about food. I always try to respond to everyone. In my program I never use the expression "I'm teaching" because people have their own way of cooking, of interpreting a recipe. I always say "Today I have something new, let's see if you like it, it really is very good." Even now I enjoy trying out new recipes. My family – my daughter Beth, my son-in-law Antonio Jorge and especially my beloved grandchildren, Rodrigo and Juliana – are my main guinea-pigs. These

past years goodness knows how many things they have tried, tasted or disapproved of. I have a great deal of respect for their opinion and that of my friends. You need to be humble.

When I go down to Santos, my grandchildren always greet me with a list: "Granny, I want honey-cake to eat." And I don't argue. Cooking for me is a pleasure and eating even more so. I love a good joint of stuffed lamb and all kinds of pastry dishes. I also adore desserts, especially meringues, soufflés and seasonal fruit pies.

In 1976 I published my first book *Ofélia's wonderful kitchen*. Since then there have been many more. During my trips around Brazil, signing books and attending festivals, I have collected a lot of recipes. Our cuisine is so delicious! I always say that our roots are very good: Portuguese, African and native Brazilian. This book demonstrates the whole range of flavors, aromas and seasonings of the Brazilian kitchen. It is an anthology of my best recipes from our culinary heritage. I hope you like them.

Ofélia

Para Começar

6 cups/1kg black-eye beans

Salt

1 large onion, grated

Palm oil for frying

For the filling:

2 finely chopped long red peppers

1 cup/200g dried shrimp

1 finely chopped onion

Salt

2 tbsp/30ml palm oil

Put the beans to soak in a bowl of water overnight. The next day put them through a mincer or a food processor. Season with salt and mix to a smooth paste with the onion, using a wooden spoon. Take tablespoonfuls of the mixture and fry in very hot palm oil. Drain the patties on absorbent paper.

To prepare the filling: put the pepper, shrimp and onion through the mincer or food processor. Season with salt. Heat the palm oil in a pan, add the shrimp mixture and cook for 5 minutes. Split the patties through the middle and fill with the shrimp mixture.

Suggestion: if you don't want a very hot filling, make a milder one with 1 cup of minced dried shrimp, 1 grated onion, 2 cloves of garlic, black pepper, and cumin. Cook in palm oil.

Makes: 40 patties

# "Acarajé"
# (Bean patties)

1 pound/500g fresh or frozen crab meat

Salt and pepper

Lemon juice

2 large grated onions

3 cloves garlic

3 tomatoes, skinned and chopped

2 tbsp/30ml olive oil

1 tbsp/15ml palm oil

1 bunch chopped coriander

Hot pepper sauce

Nutmeg

2 eggs, beaten

6 slices of bread soaked in milk

Breadcrumbs

2 tbsp/50g grated Parmesan

Butter

12 scallop shells

# Crab gratin

Thaw the crab meat if frozen. Wash and flake in a sieve to drain off all the water. Season with salt, pepper, and lemon juice. Leave it to marinade for 30 minutes. Then fry the onion, garlic, and tomatoes in the olive and palm oils. Add the crab meat and mix with a wooden spoon. Add the coriander, pepper sauce, nutmeg, and eggs. Squeeze out the slices of bread and add to the mixture. Continue stirring until a firm consistency is obtained.

Fill the scallop shells with the mixture. Sprinkle with breadcrumbs and grated cheese. Place a knob of butter on top of each shell. Place in a preheated hot oven (425 °F/220 °C) and cook until they are golden brown.

Note: if you don't have suitable shells, grill the mixture in a greased ovenproof dish.

Makes: 12 shells

# Shrimp patties

For the pastry:

4 cups/500g flour

1 cup/250g butter or margarine at room temperature

Salt and 1 cup/250ml of water

For the filling:

3 cups/600g shrimp

2 grated onions

4 chopped tomatoes

Oil

Salt and pepper

2 tbsp/30g flour

Butter, margarine or oil to grease the dish

1 egg yolk

To prepare the pastry: place the flour in a bowl. Make a well in the middle and rub in the butter or margarine. Stir in the salt and mix to a dough with water and then knead with the hands until it is smooth.

To prepare the filling: sauté the shrimp, onion, and tomato in the oil for 5 minutes. Season with salt and pepper. Reduce the heat and add the flour. Stir until it thickens a little. Grease individual molds 2½ inches/6 cm in diameter. Line them with the pastry, put in the filling and cover them with another layer of pastry. Glaze with egg yolk. Bake in a preheated moderate oven (350 °F/180 °C) until they are golden brown.

Suggestion: for a change fill the patties with palm hearts, chicken, etc.

Makes: 25 patties

# Oven turnovers

For the filling:

Diced cheese

Salt

Oregano

For the pastry:

3 cups/375g flour

1 tbsp/25g baking powder

½ cup/100g butter or margarine at room temperature

Salt

½ tin unsweetened condensed milk

¼ cup/60ml milk

1 egg to glaze

Butter, oil or margarine to grease the dish

To prepare the filling: season the cheese with salt and oregano. Put aside.

To prepare the pastry: sieve the flour and baking powder together in a bowl. Add the butter or margarine and the salt. Beat with a fork, gradually adding sufficient cream and milk to form a soft dough. Place on a floured surface, knead lightly to form a ball. Roll out, place the filling on the pastry (about 1 teaspoon for each turnover) and shape turnovers about 2½ inches/6 cm long. To prevent them from opening, paint the beaten egg along the edges of the pastry and seal them with a fork. Place them on a greased baking tray and glaze with egg. Place in a moderate oven (350 °F/180 °C) until the turnovers are golden brown.

Makes: 35 turnovers

# Fish loaf

4 cups/1kg flaked cooked fish

1 cup/125g breadcrumbs

1 cup/250ml melted butter or margarine

1 cup/100g chopped chives

1 cup/100g chopped parsley

Salt and pepper

Juice of 2 lemons

2 tsp/10g baking powder

Oil to grease the tin


Mix all the ingredients together well. Place the mixture in a loaf tin (10 x 5½ x 2½ inches/25 x 14 x 7cm). Bake in a preheated oven (425 °F/220 °C) for 35 minutes. Leave to cool and serve in slices.


Serves 8 people

# Savory squid

3 or 4 large squid or 1 octopus (5 lb/2kg)

Juice of 3 lemons

3 cloves garlic, crushed

½ cup/125ml oil

1 bunch coriander, chopped

1 tbsp/15ml red wine vinegar

Salt and pepper

Oregano


Clean the squid well. Coat with lemon juice and boil in unsalted water for 30 minutes. Drain. Leave to cool and cut into small pieces.

Fry the garlic in the oil. Add the squid. Reduce the heat, adding half the coriander, the vinegar, and the salt. Leave to simmer for 2 minutes. Season with pepper and oregano. Remove from the heat and add the remainder of the coriander. Serve on slices of bread.


Serves 6 to 8 people

# Pumpkin soup

2 cloves of garlic, crushed

2 onions, finely chopped

¼ cup/60ml oil

1 medium-sized pumpkin (2½ lb/1kg), cut in pieces

8 cups/2 l meat stock (see recipe on p. 28)

1 heaped tbsp/30g flour

1 cup/250ml milk

Salt and pepper

1 tbsp/15g chives, finely chopped

Grated Parmesan or similar cheese, to dust

Fry the garlic and the onion in the oil. Add the pumpkin and the meat stock. Reduce the heat and leave to simmer until the pumpkin is soft. Strain through a coarse sieve. Return to the heat, add the flour dissolved in the milk and season with salt and pepper. Stir until the soup is creamy. Add the chives. When it begins to bubble, remove from the heat. When serving sprinkle with the grated cheese.

Serves 6

# Watercress soup

1 bunch of watercress

1 large onion, chopped

2 cloves of garlic

4 cooked potatoes

1 cup/250ml water

8 cups/2 l meat stock (see recipe on p. 28)

Salt

Pinch of nutmeg

Wash the watercress well. Put the watercress, onion, garlic, potato, and water through the food processor or liquidizer. Combine the watercress mixture and the meat stock in a pan. Season with salt and nutmeg. Leave to simmer over a low heat for 20 minutes.

Serves 6

# Cassava soup

2 cloves of garlic, crushed

2 onions, finely chopped

1 tbsp/15g butter

8 cups/2 l meat stock (see recipe below)

3 cups/800g cassava, chopped

Chopped parsley to garnish

Fry the garlic and the onions in the butter. Add the meat stock and the cassava. Reduce the heat, cover the pan and leave to simmer until the cassava disintegrates and the soup is thickened. Garnish with a sprinkling of parsley.

Serves 6

# Bean soup with vegetables

3 ladlefuls of light brown beans, cooked

3 small carrots, finely chopped

1 large turnip, chopped

1 cup/150g green beans, finely chopped

1 cup/100g fresh herbs, finely chopped

8 cups/2 l meat stock (see recipe below)

Salt

Mix all the ingredients together in a pan and bring to a boil. Cover the pan and leave it to simmer over a low heat for 20 minutes.

Serves 6

# Meat stock

6 cups/1kg stewing beef, in pieces

16 cups/4 l water

1 large onion, chopped

1 clove garlic

1 tomato

1 bunch of mixed herbs, tied

Salt and pepper

Place all the ingredients in a pan. Boil until the liquid is reduced by half. Leave to cool, remove the meat and the herbs. Put the remainder through the food processor or the liquidizer.

For the chicken stock:

1 chicken carcass

4 cups/1 l water

1 ginger root, sliced

2 tbsp/30ml soy sauce

Salt

3 cups/750ml chicken stock

2 tbsp/30ml soy sauce

10 slices ginger

1 stem of lemon verbena, finely chopped

2 fresh mushrooms, sliced

6 tips fresh asparagus

1 tsp/5ml pepper sauce

6 large shrimp, shelled and cleaned

Juice of 2 lemons

Coriander leaves to garnish

Prepare the chicken stock: place all the ingredients in a pan and bring to a boil. Reduce the heat, cover the pan and simmer for 1 hour. Remove from the heat and strain off the stock.

Return the stock to the pan and add the soy sauce, the ginger, the lemon verbena, the mushrooms, and the asparagus. Place on the heat and bring to the boil. Add the pepper sauce, the shrimp, and the lemon juice. Reduce the heat and cook for a further 5 minutes. Remove from the heat. Serve immediately, garnished with coriander leaves.

Serves 2

# Spicy shrimp

soup

# Rice with cashew nuts

2 cups/500g rice

2 onions, finely chopped

4 cloves garlic, crushed

1 tbsp/15g chives, finely chopped

1 tbsp/15g parsley, finely chopped

3 tbsp/45g butter or margarine

1 cup/300g ground beef

1 cup/300g ground pork

1 cup/250ml tomato purée

Salt and pepper

½ cup/100g ham, chopped

½ cup/60g seedless raisins

1 tin peas

2 cups/250g cashew nuts, chopped

3 tbsp/75g grated Parmesan cheese


Boil the rice according to the instructions on the packet. In a separate pan fry the onion, garlic, chives, and parsley in the butter or margarine. Add the ground meat and the tomato purée. Season with salt and pepper. Reduce the heat and leave to simmer for 20 minutes, stirring the meat occasionally.

When the rice is almost dry, add the fried meat, ham, raisins, peas, and cashew nuts. Stir, cover the pan and leave for a few minutes. Arrange the rice on a serving dish and sprinkle with the grated cheese.


Serves 12

# Rice with coconut

2 cups/500g rice

2 cups/500ml boiling water

Salt

1½ cups/400ml coconut milk


Wash the rice. Place in a pan and add the water. Season with salt. Cover the pan and simmer until the rice is almost dry. Add the coconut milk and cook a little longer until the rice has a creamy consistency.


Serves 4 to 5

1 onion, finely chopped

2 cloves garlic, finely chopped

1 pinch paprika

1 cup/250ml oil

Chicken, 1 breast, 1 thigh and 1 drumstick, cooked and boned

1 smoked sausage, sliced

1 cup/200g smoked pork fillet, chopped

1 cup/200g roast meat, shredded

Salt and pepper

3 cups/750g rice

1 chayote, finely chopped

1 carrot, sliced

1 cup/150g green beans, finely chopped

1 small cabbage, cut into 8 pieces

1 red pepper, finely chopped

1 bunch fresh herbs, chopped

# "Braga rice"

Fry the onion, garlic, and paprika in the oil. Add the chicken, the sausage, the pork fillet, and the roast meat. Season with salt and pepper. Fry for a few minutes. Add the rice and fry a little longer. Add the chayote, carrot, beans, and cabbage. Add sufficient boiling water to cover the rice. Cook until the rice is soft and moist. If necessary add more water. Remove from the heat, sprinkle the pepper on top and garnish with the herbs.

Note: a lot of people think that "Braga rice" is a Portuguese dish. In fact it is a Brazilian recipe, but it was possibly invented in Brazil by a Portuguese whose name was Braga.

Serves 15

# Spiced rice

1 bunch sorrel

Salt

2 onions, finely chopped

2 tomatoes, finely chopped

3 cloves garlic, crushed

1 bunch coriander, finely chopped

1 red pepper

2 tbsp/30g pork fat

5 cups/1kg dried shrimp, shelled

1 cup/125g roast sesame seed

1 cup/125g cassava flour

1½ cups/250g okra, chopped

2 cups/500g rice

Boil the sorrel in salted water. Save the cooking water. On a wooden board finely chop the sorrel with a knife.
In a large skillet fry the onion, tomato, garlic, coriander, and red pepper in the pork fat. Add the shrimp and the sesame seed. Gradually add the cassava flour mixed with the water in which the sorrel was cooked. Stir continuously. Add the okra. Keep stirring until a smooth sauce is formed.
Prepare plain white rice. Arrange on a serving dish and pour the sauce over it.

Serves 6 to 8

# Carter's rice

12 cups/2kg dried meat in large pieces

2 cups/250g bacon, finely chopped

2 large onions, finely chopped

2 tomatoes, skinned and without seeds, finely chopped

1 cup/100g fresh herbs, finely chopped

1 bay leaf

2 cups/500g rice

Salt and pepper

2 cups/250g smoked pork sausage, finely chopped

Leave the dried meat to soak overnight in cold water. Change the water a few times. The next day cut the meat in small pieces and boil. Throw the water away. In a large skillet, fry the bacon over a low heat. Turn up the heat, add the onion, tomato, herbs, and bay leaf. Fry gently for a few minutes. Add the dried meat. Keep stirring for a few more minutes and if necessary add a little water. Reduce the heat and cover the pan. Cook until the meat is tender. Add the rice and stir for about 5 minutes until it has absorbed the flavors. Season with salt and pepper. Add the sausage. Add boiling water, cover and leave to simmer for about 30 minutes.

Suggestion: if possible cook the rice in a ceramic or stone pot in which it can be placed on the table and serve sprinkled with crackling crumbs.

Serves 15

# Seafood risotto

1 octopus (2½ lb/1kg)

9-10 cups (2kg) small or medium shrimp

2 tbsp/30g butter or margarine

8 cups/2kg clean mussels

2 or 3 squid (2½ lb/1kg) cut into rings

8 tomatoes, skinned and without seeds, finely chopped

2 red peppers, finely chopped

Cumin

Salt

1 bottle dry white wine

5 onions, grated

6 cloves garlic, crushed

3 tbsp/45ml oil

4 cups/1kg rice (preferably parboiled)

4 cups/1 l meat stock (see recipe on p. 28)

Grated Parmesan cheese

Clean the octopus and wash it well. Boil it in unsalted water, so that it does not get hard, for 30 minutes. Cut into small pieces and set aside.

Clean the shrimp. In a large pan melt the butter or margarine and sauté the shrimp quickly, without crisping. Add the mussels, squid, tomatoes, pepper, and cumin. Season with salt. Add 1 cup (250ml) of wine and cook for 5 minutes. Set aside.

Fry the onion and garlic in the oil. Add the rice. Fry for a few minutes more. Season with salt. Add enough boiling water to cover and cook until the rice is dry.

Add the rice and the octopus to the seafood mixture. Gradually add the meat stock and the remainder of the wine by turn and complete the cooking, stirring continuously for about 30 minutes. The risotto should be moist and the rice al dente. Serve sprinkled with the grated cheese.

Serves 20

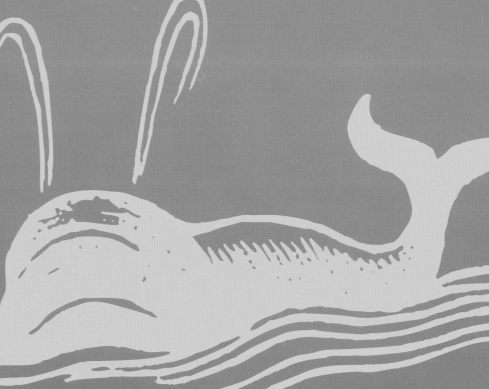

# Peixes

# Navy blue

9–10 cups/2kg flaked fish

1 bunch coriander, finely chopped

1 bunch fresh herbs, finely chopped

Juice of 4 lemons

4 cloves garlic, crushed

Salt and pepper

4 large onions, sliced

12 tomatoes, skinned and finely chopped

½ cup/125ml oil

2 cups/500ml boiling water

5 cups/1kg medium shrimp, shelled and chopped

Long red pepper, finely chopped


For the banana mush:

2 dozen small green bananas

1½ cups/375ml fish stock

Coarse ground cassava flour


In a large bowl combine the flaked fish, coriander, fresh herbs, juice of 3 lemons, 3 cloves of garlic, salt, and pepper. Leave to marinade for 1 hour.

Fry the onion and 3 tomatoes in half the oil. Add the fish. Reduce the heat, add the boiling water and leave to simmer for 15 to 20 minutes. Set aside the fish stock. Season the shrimp with the remaining garlic, salt and pepper, and the juice of 1 lemon, then fry in the remaining oil. Add the remaining tomatoes and cook for a few minutes. Add the long red pepper and stir. Set aside.

Prepare the mush: peel the bananas, take out the 'strings' and cover them with water and cook. Remove from the heat and drain. Mash with a fork, add the fish stock and mix well. Return to the heat and add the cassava flour, stirring continuously to thicken until a soft mush is formed.

Serve the flaked fish with the shrimp sauce accompanied by the banana mush.


Serves 10

2½ cups/500g cod in pieces

2½ cups/500g green papaya

1 large onion, finely chopped

1 clove garlic, crushed

1 bay leaf

1 cup/100g coriander, finely chopped

1 small pepper, finely chopped

2 tomatoes, finely chopped

1 tbsp/15ml palm oil

2 tbsp/30ml corn oil

¾ cup/200ml coconut milk or the milk from 1 large coconut

1 cup fresh cream

# Cod with coconut
## and papaya

Put the cod to soak overnight in cold water. Change the water
a few times.

The next day, peel the papaya and cut it in even pieces. Poach
the cod, skin and bone it. Cut into slices.

Fry the onion, garlic, bay leaf, coriander, pepper, and tomato in
the palm oil and corn oil for a few minutes. Add the cod and
papaya. Stir carefully so as not to break up the fish. Mix the
coconut milk with the cream and add to the cod. Reduce the
heat, cover the pan and leave to simmer for 10 minutes. Serve
with white rice.

Serves 4

15 corn cobs

3 cups/750ml water

2 chicken stock cubes

5 cups/1kg shrimp with shell

1 large onion, grated

8 large tomatoes, skinned and chopped

2 tbsp/30ml oil

1 bunch fresh herbs, finely chopped

1 bay leaf

Salt and black pepper

For the mush:

2 cups/500ml milk

1 scant cup/200ml coconut milk

3 heaped tbsp/60g rice flour

Salt

# Corn

Scrape the corn from the cobs. Pulp the grains in the blender with 1 cup of water. Sieve. Measure the quantity of the paste and add an equal quantity of water. Cook over a low heat, stirring continuously, and add the chicken stock cubes. Leave to thicken a little and set aside.

Boil the heads and shells of the shrimp in 2 cups of salted water. Strain the stock and reserve. Fry the onion and tomato in the oil. Add the shrimp stock, herbs, bay leaf, and black pepper. Add the shrimp and season with salt. Reduce the heat and leave to simmer for 15 minutes. Add the corn paste, stir and allow to heat through.

Prepare the mush: mix all the ingredients in a pan and stir well until they form a soft mush. Serve with the hotpot.

Serves 12

cob hotpot

1 ripe medium squash

Salt and pepper

2 cloves garlic, crushed

5 cups/1kg small shrimp

Juice of 2 lemons

1 large onion, grated

2 tbsp/30g butter or margarine

1 cup/100g coriander, finely chopped

1 tbsp/15g cornflour

1 cup/250ml milk

2 tbsp/30ml ketchup

1 cup/250ml tomato purée

1 catupiri or other soft cheese

Large shrimp to garnish

# Squash

Wash the outside of the squash, rubbing it to get rid of any dirt or earth. Cut a lid from it and set aside. Clean the inside, taking out the seeds and core. Season the inside with salt, pepper, and garlic.

Season the shrimp with salt and lemon. Sauté the onion in the butter or margarine. Add the shrimp and coriander. Season with black pepper. Reduce the heat and leave to simmer for 10 minutes. Dissolve the cornflour in the milk. Add to the shrimp mixture, stirring until it thickens. Add the ketchup and tomato purée, mixing well. Reserve. Turn the squash upside down to drain off excess liquid. Put in a layer of the crumbled cheese, then top with shrimp mixture. Put the lid on and roast in a roasting dish in a preheated moderate oven (350 °F/180 °C) until soft. Remove from the oven and decorate with large shrimp cooked in their shells. Serve with white rice.

Serves 6 to 8

stuffed with shrimp

1 large gilthead (or 'dorado') (5 lb/2kg), cleaned and
slit lengthwise
Salt and pepper
2 cloves garlic, crushed
Juice of 1 lemon

# Gilthead fried in

For the stuffing:
2 onions, grated
2 carrots, grated
2 tomatoes, skinned and finely chopped
1 cup/250g butter or margarine
1 cup/100g coriander, finely chopped
Salt
½ cup/130g toasted cassava flour
2 cups/500ml fish bone stock

1 banana leaf
Oil for basting

Stitch together the lower part of the fish, leaving an
open pocket. Make a paste with the salt, pepper, garlic,
and lemon juice and rub the fish with it inside and out.
Leave to marinate for 1 hour.
Boil the fish bones in salted water, strain and reserve.
Prepare the stuffing: fry the onion, carrot, and tomato in
the butter or margarine. Add the coriander and season
with salt. Add the cassava flour and fish stock and stir for
a few minutes.
Stuff the fish with the stuffing, stitch up the opening and
leave to stand for 1 hour. Reserve some of the stuffing.
Wilt the banana leaf in the oven for 1 or 2 minutes. Baste
with oil and wrap the fish in it. Place in a preheated hot
oven (425 °F/220 °C) for 1 hour. Serve the fish in thick
slices with the remainder of the stuffing.

Serves 6 to 8

a banana leaf

2 fresh lobsters

Salt and pepper

Juice of 1 lemon

2 onions, sliced

2 cloves garlic, crushed

5 ripe tomatoes, skinned and without seeds

½ cup/125ml olive oil

1 bunch coriander, finely chopped

2 cups/500ml coconut milk

½ cup/125ml palm oil

1 long red pepper, finely chopped

Cut the lobster meat in large pieces. Season with salt, pepper, and lemon. In a pan, fry the onion, garlic, and tomato in the olive oil. Add the lobster and fry for a few more minutes. Add the coriander, coconut milk, and palm oil. Mix well. Reduce the heat and leave to simmer for 20 to 25 minutes.

Before serving add the long red pepper.

Serves 4

# Lobster hotpot

20–24 cups/4kg fish (grouper or namorado)

Juice of 5 lemons

Salt and pepper

6 onions, finely chopped

3 cloves garlic, crushed

1 cup/100g fresh herbs, finely chopped

2 tbsp/30g basil, finely chopped

1 cup/100g coriander, finely chopped

3 tomatoes, skinned and without seeds, finely chopped

1 red pepper, finely chopped and crushed

1 cup/250ml palm oil

½ cup/125ml olive oil

2¼ cups/600ml coconut milk

# Fish hotpot

Cut the fish into slices, discarding the heads. Season with lemon, salt, and pepper. Cover and leave to marinate for 30 minutes.

Fry the onion, garlic, herbs, basil, coriander, tomato, and pepper in the palm oil and olive oil. Add the slices of fish, stir and fry a little longer. Add the coconut milk. Reduce the heat, cover the pan and cook for 20 minutes. Do not stir again, to avoid breaking up the fish. Serve with rice with coconut (see recipe on p. 32).

Suggestion: if you like, serve with pepper sauce made with long red pepper marinaded in palm oil.

Serves 16

5 cups/1kg fish, sliced and boned

(grouper, namorado or shark)

1 heaped cup/250g cleaned shrimp

1 cup/250g oysters boiled in salted water

1 cup/250g dressed crab

1 cup/250g clams

Salt and pepper

Juice of 3 lemons

1 long red pepper, finely chopped

1 cup/250ml oil

1 pinch annatto or 2 tsp orange colorant

3 cloves garlic, crushed

4 onions, sliced

4 cups/1kg tomatoes, skinned and without seeds, finely chopped

1 bunch coriander, finely chopped

1 tin palm hearts in slices

1 cup/150g pitted black olives, finely chopped

12 eggs, separated

Season the fish, shrimp, oysters, crab, and clams with the salt, pepper, lemon, and long red pepper. Heat the oil in a large pan, add the annatto and fry for 1 minute. Add the garlic, onion, and tomato and fry until the onion softens. Reduce the heat, add the fish and simmer for 10 minutes. Add the shellfish and simmer for a further 5 minutes. Finally add the coriander, palm hearts, and olives. Mix well and remove from the heat. Whisk 8 egg whites until they form peaks. Add 8 yolks and beat a little longer. Add the whole to the fish and shellfish mixture. Place in a rectangular earthenware or ovenproof dish. Whisk the other 4 eggs until frothy and cover the whole surface of the dish with them. Cook in a preheated moderate oven (350 °F/180 °C) until the pie is golden brown.

Serves 8 to 10

# Fisherman's pie

10-12 cups/2kg fish in slices

(shark, swordfish, namorado or grouper)

Salt

Juice of 2 lemons

2 cloves garlic, crushed

1½ cups/300g fresh medium shrimp, cleaned

1 cup/250ml olive oil

1½ cups/300g dried unsalted shrimp

3 tomatoes, skinned and without seeds,

finely chopped

1½ cups/200g cashew nuts

1½ cups/200g peanuts, shelled and roasted

4 onions, finely chopped

4 cloves garlic, crushed

1 cup/125g rice flour

3 cups/750ml coconut milk

5 tbsp/75ml palm oil

Season the fish with salt, lemon, and garlic. Reserve. Fry the fresh shrimp quickly in the olive oil. Reserve. Wash the dried shrimp and boil for 5 minutes. Remove from the heat and strain, reserving the liquid. Cook the fish for 15 minutes with the seasoning in which it was marinating, the tomato, and a little water. Reserve. Put the dried shrimp, cashew nuts, peanuts, onion, and garlic through the mincer or food processor. Mix this paste into the reserved liquid and cook over a low heat. Dissolve the rice flour in the coconut milk. Incorporate this mixture into the vatapá, stirring continuously until it thickens. Add the palm oil. Add the sliced fish (with the stock) and the fresh shrimp and leave on the heat for a further 5 minutes. Serve very hot with rice with coconut (see recipe on p. 32).

Note: if the dry shrimp is salted, leave it to soak for 3 hours, changing the water several times

Serves 8 to 10

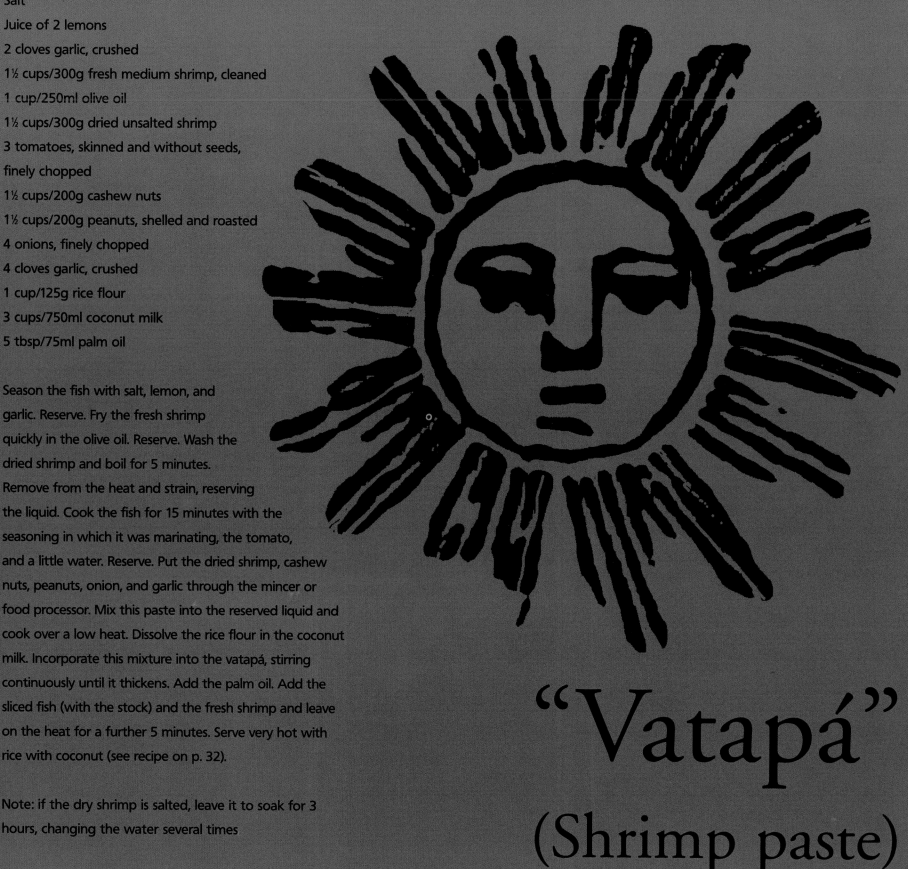

# "Vatapá"
# (Shrimp paste)

OCEAN I

# Shrimp and okra stew ("Zorô")

5 cups/1kg shrimp, in their shells

Salt and pepper

Juice of 1 lemon

1 onion, finely chopped

3 cloves garlic, crushed

4 tomatoes, finely chopped

3 stems of coriander

1 bunch fresh herbs

1 red pepper, finely chopped

½ cup/125ml olive oil

2 tbsp/30ml palm oil

6–7 cups/1kg okra, finely sliced

For the mush:

Shrimp stock

Corn meal

Salt

Boil the shells and heads of the shrimp. Reserve the stock. Season the shrimp with salt, pepper, and lemon. Put the onion, garlic, tomato, coriander, herbs, and pepper through the liquidizer or food processor. Fry for 5 minutes in the olive and palm oils. Add the shrimp and fry for a further 2 minutes. Add the okra. Reduce the heat, cover the pan and simmer for 10 minutes. Prepare the mush: take the shrimp stock and boil. Add the corn meal gradually, stirring vigorously. Season with salt. Cook, stirring continuously, until the mush is very soft and well cooked. Serve with the stew.

Serves 6

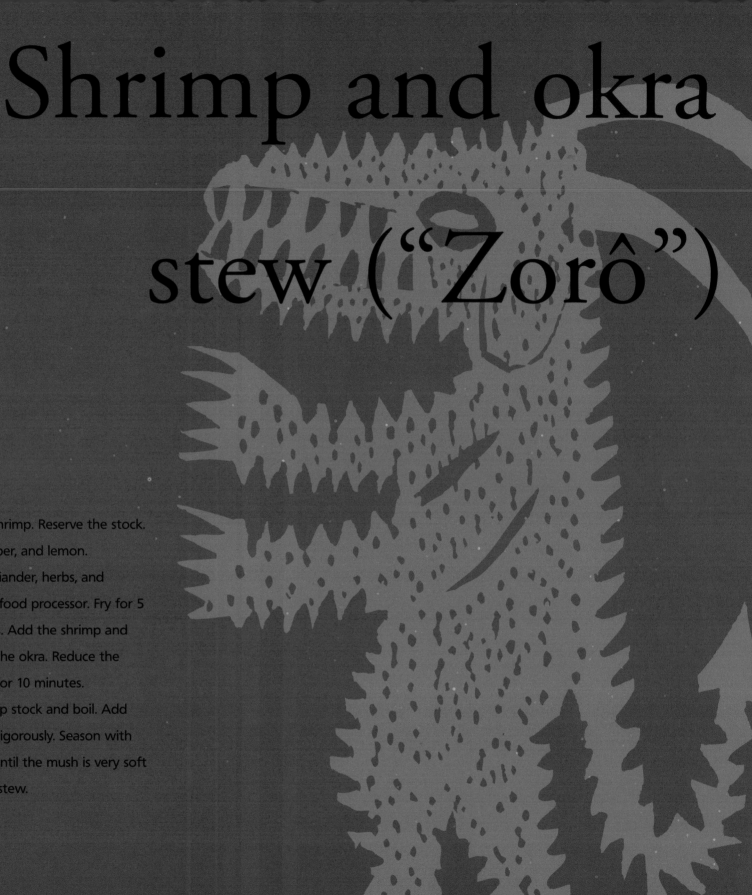

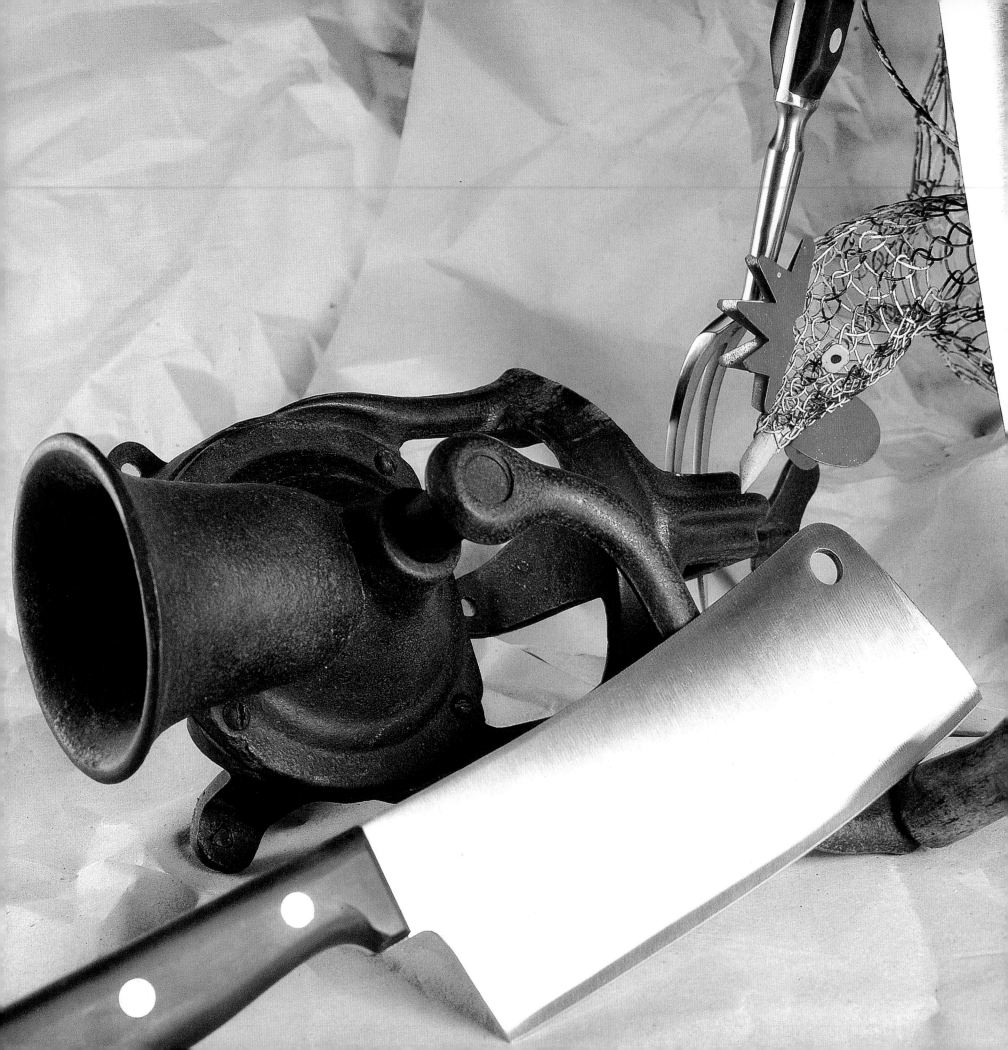

# Carnes

3 cups/500g dried meat, in pieces

2 cups/300g salt pork fillet, in pieces

3 cups/450g light brown beans

4 cabanos, thickly sliced

4 pork sausages, thickly sliced

1 cup/200g bacon, finely chopped

3 cups/750g rice

4 onions, finely chopped

4 cloves garlic, crushed

Salt

1 bunch fresh herbs, finely chopped

Cumin

½ cup/125ml oil

1 cup/250g mild cheese, chopped

1–2 cups/250g pork crackling

For the "farofa" (to sprinkle on):

3 onions, finely chopped

½ to ¾ cup/100-150g butter

6 small green bananas, in pieces

Cassava flour

Salt and pepper

Soak the dried meat and salt pork overnight. Pick over the beans and wash them well. Cook with the dried meat, salt pork, cabanos, sausages, and bacon, with sufficient water to cover. After 40 minutes add the rice. Fry the onion, garlic, salt, herbs, and cumin in the oil. Add this to the rice and beans. Mix. Cover the pan and leave to simmer for a further 30 minutes. Top up with boiling water whenever necessary. Add the cheese.

Prepare the "farofa": fry the onion in the butter. Add the banana and fry for a few minutes more. Add the cassava flour. Keep stirring for a few minutes. Season with salt and pepper. Serve the stew with some pork crackling.

Note: to prepare the crackling, cut the fresh belly pork into large pieces and fry in its own fat until it is crisp. Drain on absorbent paper.

Serves 12 to 15

# Pork and beef hotpot

4 tomatoes, skinned and with seeds removed, finely chopped

4 onions, finely chopped

4 cloves garlic, crushed

3 bay leaves

Cumin

1 long red pepper, finely chopped and crushed

1 bunch herbs, finely chopped

12 cups/2kg rump steak, in pieces

6 cups/1kg stewing steak, in pieces

2½ cups/500g diced bacon

½ cup/125ml white wine vinegar

½ cup/125ml oil

For the layering:
Cassava flour and water

In a large bowl mix together the tomato, onion, garlic, bay leaf, cumin, pepper, and herbs. In an earthenware or stoneware dish, place a layer of the two meats mixed together, a layer of seasoning, and a layer of bacon. Repeat the layers until the ingredients are used up. Pour over the vinegar and the oil. Place the lid on and leave to stand overnight. The next day make a paste with the cassava flour and water. "Seal" the dish by plugging the gap between the dish and the lid with the cassava paste. Cook over a low heat for about 4 hours. If any steam escapes, seal the gap with a little more of the paste. Serve with white rice or "farofa" (see p.64).

The writer and gourmet Antônio Houaiss is convinced that the sealed cooking pot was the precursor of the pressure cooker.

Serves 12 to 15

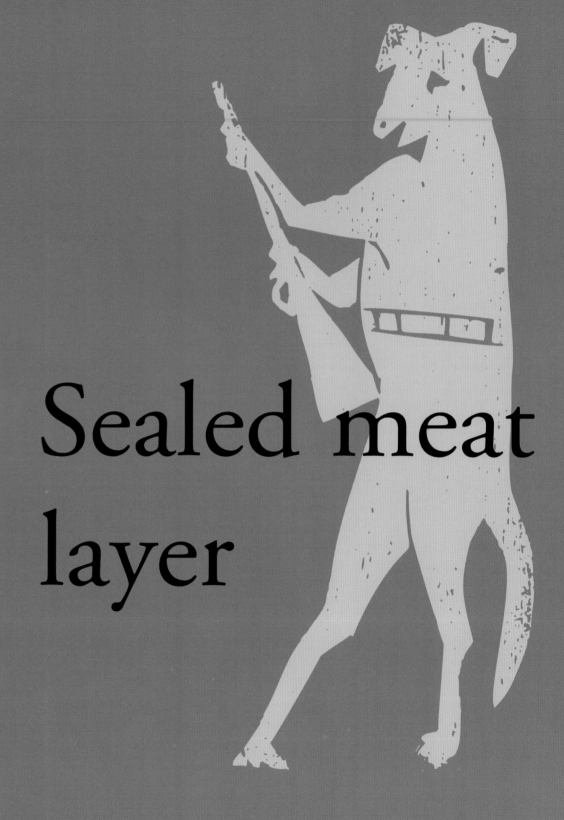

# Sealed meat layer

8 cups/1.5kg dried meat (lean) in pieces

1 tbsp/15g crushed garlic

1 cup/250ml oil

Bay leaves

2 tomatoes, skinned and without seeds

3 onions, sliced

2 tbsp/30g chives, finely chopped

Salt and pepper

For the pumpkin mush:

1 tsp/7g crushed garlic

2 onions, finely chopped

1 cup/250ml oil

8 cups/2kg ripe pumpkin, in pieces

Salt and pepper

Finely chopped parsley

Finely chopped chives

# Dried meat with pumpkin

Bring the dried meat to the boil in a pan of water. Change the water then leave to soak overnight. Rinse the meat well and boil until tender. Remove from the pan and drain. Fry the garlic in the oil until golden. Add the dried meat, bay leaves, and tomato and fry for a few minutes more. Add the onion and the chives. Stir, frying gently for a few minutes or until the onion is soft. Season with salt and pepper.

Prepare the mush: in a pan fry the garlic and onion in oil. Add the pumpkin. Season with salt and pepper. Cover the pan and leave to cook over a low heat, drizzling with hot water occasionally. The pumpkin should soften but not disintegrate. Sprinkle with parsley and chives. Serve with the dried meat.

Serves 8

1 cup/150g green pepper, finely chopped

6 ripe tomatoes, chopped

1 large onion, finely chopped

2 cups/500ml oil

5 lb/2kg osso bucco

Salt

Pepper sauce

Flour

For the mush:

Meat stock

4 cups/500g cassava flour

# Beef stew

In a skillet fry the pepper, tomato, and onion in half the oil until soft. Reserve. Season the pieces of osso bucco with salt and pepper sauce. Toss in the flour and fry in the remainder of the oil, browning on both sides.
Add the meat to the tomato mixture. Cover with hot water and leave to simmer over a low heat for about 1 hour or until tender.
Prepare the mush: take almost all the liquid from the meat and place in a pan. Add the cassava flour gradually and cook, stirring continuously until a soft mush is obtained. Serve with the osso bucco.

Serves 6

# Brazilian-style hotpot

6 cups/1kg stewing steak in pieces

2 cloves garlic, crushed

Salt and pepper

3 cups/500g smoked pork fillet

4 pork sausages, sliced

3 cups/500g cured or smoked sausage, in pieces

Salt

1 bay leaf

1 red pepper, finely chopped

1 bunch fresh herbs, tied

Cumin

1 cup/250g diced bacon

3 cassavas, in pieces

5 sweet potatoes, in pieces

5 cooking bananas

1 piece ripe pumpkin, cut in large cubes

1 small cabbage, cut in four

5 carrots, sliced

2 white turnips, in pieces

1 small cauliflower, separated into florets

A few leaves of collard

6 whole onions

5 hard-boiled eggs

Oil for dressing


For the mush:

Stock

Coarse cassava flour

Salt and pepper

Season the meat the night before with the garlic, salt, and pepper.

In a large pan, with plenty of water, bring the stewing steak, smoked pork, pork sausage, and smoked sausage to the boil. Season with salt. Add the bay leaf, pepper, and bunch of fresh herbs. Add the cumin and the bacon. Reduce the heat, cover and simmer for about 1 hour, until the meat is tender. Boil the cassava, sweet potato, and bananas, in their skins, separately. Add to the pan with the meat the pumpkin, cabbage, carrots, turnip, cauliflower, and collard leaves. Cover the pan and simmer over a low heat. After 10 minutes add the onions. Remove the vegetables as they cook and put aside, keeping them warm.

Prepare the mush: take some stock from the cooking pot. Allow to cool a little. Place on the heat and gradually add the cassava flour. Season with salt and pepper. Boil, stirring continuously, until it thickens. Serve up the meat separately with a little stock accompanied by the vegetables, the halved hard-boiled eggs and the peeled bananas. Drizzle the oil over the meat and vegetables. Serve with the mush.

Serves 10 to 15

1 piece of "cupim"

2 bay leaves

Salt

3 tbsp/45ml oil

Juice of 2 lemons

Pepper

1 red pepper, finely chopped and pounded

3 tbsp/45ml Worcester sauce

1 cup/250ml red wine

1 bunch rosemary

4 tbsp/60ml oil

6 cups/1kg small potatoes, peeled

Wash the meat. Place it with the bay leaf, salt, and oil in a pressure cooker, with enough water to cover. Cook for 1½ hours. Remove the meat from the pressure cooker. Season with lemon juice, pepper, red pepper, Worcester sauce, and wine. Place the bunch of rosemary on top. Cover with a cloth and leave overnight.

The next day, put the meat in a roasting dish. Sprinkle with oil. Place the potatoes around it. Put in a preheated hot oven (425 °F/220 °C) and roast for 1 hour or until the meat is tender when pricked with a fork and the potatoes are browned. From time to time dip the rosemary in the wine sauce and baste the meat with it.

Serves 6

Note: the "cupim" is the hump on the back of the neck of Brahman cattle and is regarded as a great delicacy. It is very tender and flavorsome when cooked slowly.

# "Cupim" gaucho style

6 cups/1kg black beans

6 cups/1kg dried meat

2 pigs trotters

2 cups/500g pig's ear

5 pork sausages

2 cups/500g smoked sausage

2 heaped cups/600g smoked pork rib

2 cups/500g smoked pork fillet

4 cloves garlic, crushed

4 onions, finely chopped

1 bay leaf

Juice of 6 oranges

pork fillet, trotters, ear, dried meat, garlic, onions, and bay leaf. Cover the pan and simmer until the beans are soft and the meat tender. Add the smoked sausage 40 minutes after bringing to a boil. Five minutes before serving add the orange juice to the beans.

Prepare the piquant sauce: mix all the ingredients together and chill.

Prepare the greens: chop the leaves very finely. Place them in a colander and pour boiling water over them. In a large pan fry the garlic in the oil. Add the greens. Stir for a few minutes. Reduce the heat, cover the pan and leave to sweat for 5 minutes, stirring from time to time.

*Note: pronounced "fayzhwada," this is virtually the national dish of Brazil. The essential ingredients are black beans and many different kinds of meat and sausage.*

# "Feijoada" or Black bean stew

For the piquant sauce:

2 cups/500ml of the bean stock

1 red pepper, finely chopped

2 onions, grated

1 bunch fresh herbs, finely chopped

Juice of 3 lemons

For the greens:

5 heads of spring greens

6 cloves garlic, crushed

Oil

Place the beans, dried meat, pig's ear, and trotters in to soak, separately, overnight. The next day, bring the beans to the boil in a pan with plenty of water and simmer for 1 hour or cook for 20 minutes in a pressure cooker. Cut all the meat in large pieces and trim off any excess fat. Boil all the meat, drain and throw away the water. Put the beans into a large pan, add the sausage, rib,

Serve the stew with white rice and the greens with the cold sauce on the side.

Serves 8 to 10

# Chicken with cheese

1 small chicken (1kg) in pieces

Salt and pepper

Juice of 2 lemons

2 tbsp/30ml oil

1 clove garlic, crushed

1 onion, finely chopped

2 tomatoes, skinned and without seeds, finely chopped

2 cups/500ml milk

1 small soft cheese

Chives, finely chopped, to sprinkle on

Clean and season the pieces of chicken with salt, pepper,
and lemon juice. Place the oil in a pan and fry the garlic.
Add the chicken and fry for a few minutes. Add the
onion and tomato. Fry for a few minutes more. Reduce
the heat and cook the chicken with the lid on for 20
minutes. If necessary add a little water. When the chicken
is cooked, remove from the pan and take out the bones.
Cut into medium-sized pieces.
Add the milk to the sauce remaining in the pan and bring
to a boil. Add the cheese in pieces, stirring continuously,
until it reaches a creamy consistency. Put the chicken back
in the pan to heat through. Sprinkle with chives to
garnish.

Serves 4

Pork fat

1 large onion

6 cloves garlic, crushed

1 red pepper, finely chopped

1 bay leaf

1 bunch fresh herbs, finely chopped

1 piece of sucking-pig, not too fat and boned (about
7 lbs/3kg)

Salt

For the purée:
6 cups/1kg sweet
potato

Salt

3 tbsp/45g butter

Milk

# Crispy sucking-pig
## with sweet potato purée

In a very large pan heat the pork fat. Add the onion,
garlic, red pepper, bay leaf, herbs, and the sucking-pig.
Season with salt. Fry the meat on all sides until brown.
Add a little water and leave to simmer until the meat is
tender but firm. Add boiling water whenever necessary.
Remove from the heat and leave to cool. Cut the sucking-
pig into pieces. In a large skillet place the pork fat, heat
thoroughly and fry the pieces of sucking-pig until they
are well done and crispy.

Prepare the purée: boil the peeled sweet potato in salted
water. Pass through a sieve or mash with a fork. Add the
butter and mix well. Add sufficient milk to give the
required consistency. Serve the crispy sucking-pig with
the sweet potato purée.

Serves 6

1 chicken, cut into pieces

2 cloves garlic, crushed

Salt

1 cup/250ml olive oil

1 bunch fresh herbs, finely chopped

Long red peppers, minced

2 medium onions, grated

2 cups/300–400g dried shrimp, crushed

A few stems of coriander

1 tbsp/15g ginger, grated

1 cup/250ml palm oil

Season the chicken with garlic and salt. Leave to stand for 1 hour. In a pan (preferably earthenware or stoneware), sauté the pieces of chicken in the olive oil until golden. Add the herbs, red pepper, onion, shrimp, coriander, and ginger and sauté a little longer. Reduce the heat, add the palm oil and simmer over a low heat, with the lid on, for 30 minutes. If necessary add a little hot water. Serve with white rice.

Serves 6

# Chicken ragout

3 cups/500g dried meat, in pieces

2 onions, finely chopped

6 cloves garlic, crushed

½ cup/125ml olive oil

½ cup/125ml cooking oil

2 tomatoes, skinned and finely chopped

1 tin mixed vegetables, approx. 1½ cups/400g

Salt

Pepper sauce

1 cup/125g coarse cassava flour

1 cup/125g yellow cornflour

1 bunch fresh herbs, finely chopped

3 boiled eggs, chopped

Pitted black olives

# Dried meat couscous

Leave the dried meat to soak for 24 hours, changing the
water a few times. Bring to a boil and simmer for 20
minutes. Drain off the water, cut into cubes and cook in
fresh boiling water until the meat is tender. Reserve.
Sauté the onion and garlic in the olive and cooking oils.
Add the tomato, meat, and vegetables. Season with salt
and pepper sauce. Reduce the heat. Meanwhile mix the
flours and herbs in a bowl. Add this mixture to the meat,
stirring continuously. Finally mix in the eggs and olives.
Grease a 10-inch/24cm ring mold. Place the couscous in it
and level the top. Protecting your hands with a cloth,
invert the mold on a large serving dish and turn the
couscous out.

Serves 10

For the yeast mixture:

Fresh yeast

1 cup/250ml warm milk

1 tbsp/15g sugar

1 cup/125g wheatflour

For the dough:

2 cups/500g cooked and ground cassava

3 tbsp/45ml lard at room temperature

3 tbsp/45ml oil

5 beaten eggs

2 tsp/10g salt

5 cups/675g wheatflour

For the filling:

3 cups/500g ham, sliced

3 cups/500g mozzarella cheese, in slices

2 egg yolks

Grated Parmesan cheese for sprinkling

Prepare the yeast mixture: crumble the yeast in the milk. Add the sugar and flour. Mix. Leave to rise for 30 minutes. Prepare the dough: in a large bowl combine the yeast mixture, cassava, lard, oil, eggs, and salt. Add the flour. Knead the dough for 5 minutes on a floured surface. Leave the dough to prove for a further 30 minutes, with the bowl covered. Divide the dough into two. Roll out on a surface dusted with flour, place half the ham and the mozzarella on one half and roll it up. Repeat the same operation with the other half. Leave to stand for 30 minutes. Brush the roly-polys with the egg yolk and sprinkle with grated cheese. Bake in a preheated oven (350 °F/180 °C) in two greased and floured dishes, until golden brown.

Serves 12

# Cassava roly-poly

# Pumpkin soufflé

6 cups/1kg pumpkin, in pieces

Salt

1 tbsp/15ml cream or milk

3 tbsp/50g grated Parmesan cheese

3 eggs, separated

Grated Parmesan cheese for sprinkling

Steam the pumpkin until soft. Strain through a fine sieve or mash with a fork. Drain off any excess water. Season with salt. Add the cream, the Parmesan and the egg yolks. Mix well. Beat the egg whites until they form soft peaks, add to the pumpkin mixture and blend carefully. Place in a soufflé dish, 9 inches/22cm in diameter. Sprinkle with grated cheese. Place the soufflé in a preheated hot oven (425 °F/220 °C) until firm and lightly browned. Remove from the oven and serve immediately.

Serves 6

# Palm heart soufflé

2 onions, finely chopped

3 cloves garlic, crushed

2 tbsp/30g butter or margarine

2 tomatoes, skinned and finely chopped

1 tin palm hearts, sliced

Salt and pepper

½ cup/125g wheatflour

2 cups/500ml milk

4 eggs, separated

½ cup/100g Parmesan cheese, grated

Breadcrumbs

Fry the onion and garlic in half the butter or margarine. Add the tomato and palm hearts. Season with salt and pepper. Sauté for a few minutes. Reserve. Melt the remainder of the fat in a pan. Add the flour and mix. Add the milk, stirring continuously and cook until the white sauce thickens. Remove from the heat and add the egg yolks (strained), the palm heart mixture, and the Parmesan. Mix well. Beat the egg whites until they form soft peaks, add to the palm heart mixture and fold in carefully. Grease a 9-inch/22cm soufflé dish and sprinkle with breadcrumbs. Put the soufflé mixture in and cook in a preheated oven (350 °F/180° C) until firm and lightly browned. Remove from the oven and serve immediately.

Serves 6

# Chayote soufflé

2 cups/500ml milk

2 heaped tbsp/30g wheatflour

4 eggs, separated

3 tbsp/45g butter or margarine

Salt and pepper

2 cloves garlic, crushed

1 large onion

2 cups/200g ham, diced

4 cups/1kg chayote, cooked and sliced

1 cup/100g fresh herbs, finely chopped

2 heaped tbsp/50g grated Parmesan

Breadcrumbs

Mix together in a pan the milk, flour, egg yolks, and two thirds of the butter or margarine. Season with salt and pepper. Place on the heat, stirring continuously with a wooden spoon, until it thickens. Sauté the garlic and onion in the remainder of the fat and add to the white sauce. Add the ham, chayote, fresh herbs, and Parmesan. Beat the egg whites until they form soft peaks. Fold in the chayote mixture. Grease a small square or rectangular ovenproof dish and sprinkle with breadcrumbs. Pour in the soufflé mixture. Cook in a preheated oven (350 °F/180 °C) for about 20 minutes or until lightly browned. Remove from the oven and serve immediately.

Serves 8

1½ cups/375ml water

2½ cups/625g sugar

1 cup/200ml coconut milk or milk of 1 coconut

10 egg yolks

Orange flower water to taste

Mix together the water and sugar, heat without stirring until it reaches the soft ball stage. To test it, take a little of the syrup on a spoon and drop into a small bowl of cold water. When pinched between the fingers it should form a soft malleable ball. Add the coconut milk and mix well. Remove from the heat. Strain the egg yolks. Pour a little of the hot syrup over them and mix well. Add the remainder of the syrup, stirring continuously. Return to a low heat and add the orange flower water. Stir until a creamy consistency is formed. Place the Damsel's Delight in a bowl to set. Serve cold.

Serves 6

# Damsel's Delight

6 heaped tbsp/90g cornflour

2 cups/500ml milk

½ tin condensed milk

2 cups/400ml coconut milk

Extra sugar if liked

For the sweet sauce:

3 cups/750g sugar

3 cups/750ml water

2 cloves

1 piece of cinnamon

1 cup/250ml red wine

1½ cups/250g prunes

Dissolve the cornflour in the milk. Add all the other
ingredients. Strain through a sieve. Heat, stirring
continuously until it thickens. Pour the custard into a
wetted 9-inch/22cm ring mold. Leave to cool and place in
the refrigerator until it is very firm.
Prepare the sweet sauce: combine all the ingredients
together in a pan and bring to a boil until the prunes are
soft. Leave to cool. Turn out the blancmange and serve
with the sauce.

Serves 6 to 8

# Blancmange

1 tin condensed milk

12 egg yolks, strained

1 cup/200g grated coconut

2 cups/400ml coconut milk

For the syrup:

3 cups/750ml sugar

4 cups/1 l water

1 piece of cinnamon

Cream cheese or powdered cinnamon

Mix the condensed milk with the egg yolks. Reserve. Put
the grated coconut to soak in the coconut milk.
Prepare the syrup: mix the water, sugar, and cinnamon.
Heat until the syrup has the consistency of honey. Reduce
the heat. Add the coconut and milk mixture. Stir for 3
minutes over the heat. Remove from the heat and leave
to cool. Place in a custard dish. Serve with cream cheese
or sprinkled with cinnamon.

Serves 5 or 6

# Egg custard with coconut

2 cups/500ml water

2 cups/500g sugar

6 cups/1kg sweet potato, cooked and sieved/mashed

1 tsp/5ml vanilla essence

4 tbsp/60ml maraschino liqueur

Cherries to decorate

Mix the water and sugar, heat until the syrup has the consistency of honey. Add the sweet potato, vanilla essence, and maraschino. Mix well and cook, stirring continuously until the mixture comes away from the pan. Leave to cool in a bowl. Place in a serving dish and decorate with cherries.

Serves 8

# Mock "marron glacé"

with sweet potato

For the syrup:

3 cups/750ml water

1½ cups/375g sugar


7 egg yolks

1 egg white, beaten to form peaks

Butter for greasing


Prepare the syrup: combine the water and sugar, heat
without stirring until you have a thick syrup the
consistency of honey.
Beat the egg yolks thoroughly. Add the beaten white
and beat a little more. Butter 3-inch patty tins. Fill half
full. Cook in a preheated oven (350° F/180° C) for 10
minutes or until a skewer comes out clean when inserted.
Turn out the angel creams and dip them in the syrup.
Place in a bowl.


Serves 6

# Angel creams

# Papaya pudding

1 large ripe papaya

4 eggs, beaten

2 tbsp/30g wheatflour

2 tbsp/30g butter at room temperature

½ cup/125g sugar

Butter for greasing

Peel the papaya and take out the seeds. Cut into pieces and cook in sufficient water to cover until it is soft. Mash with a fork. Add the beaten eggs, flour, butter, and sugar. Butter an 8-inch/20cm ring mold. Pour the mixture into the tin. Bake in a preheated oven (425 °F/220 °C) for 20 to 25 minutes or until an inserted skewer comes out clean. Slide a knife around the edge of the mold and turn out the pudding.

Serves 8

# Cassava cake

1kg cassava

3 tbsp/45g butter or margarine at room temperature

2 cups/500ml sugar

½ cup/125g grated coconut

1 cup/200ml coconut milk

6 egg yolks

3 egg whites, beaten

½ tbsp/10g powdered yeast

Pinch of salt

Butter for greasing

Flour for sprinkling

Grate the cassava and strain through a muslin cloth (discard the juice). Put the cassava in a large bowl and add all the other ingredients. Beat well. Spoon the mixture into a 15 x 10-inch/40 x 26cm baking tin, greased and floured. Bake in a preheated moderate oven (350 °F/ 180 °C) for about 30 minutes or until an inserted skewer comes out clean. Leave to cool and cut into pieces to suit.

Serves 12

7 egg yolks

7 tbsp/105g sugar

1 tbsp/15g butter at room temperature

½ fresh coconut, grated

½ cup/125ml milk

Butter for greasing

Sugar for sprinkling

Beat the egg yolks with the sugar to obtain a pale
creamy consistency. Add the butter, coconut, and milk.
Butter individual 2½-inch/6cm dariole molds and sprinkle
with sugar, or use one 8-inch/20cm ring mold. Pour in
the mixture. Bake in a bain-marie in a hot oven
(425° F/220° C) for 40 minutes. Slide a knife round the
edge of the molds. Turn out when cold.

Serves 6

# "Quindim"

(Brazilian egg custard, pronounced "kin-ding")

# Brazil nut pie

1 cup/250g butter

2 cups/500g sugar

4 egg yolks

1 cup/250ml milk

2 cups/250g wheatflour

1 tbsp/15g powdered yeast

Butter for greasing

For the filling:

4 egg whites

1 cup/250g sugar

2 cups/250g Brazil nuts

2 cups/500ml fresh cream, whipped

Beat the butter until it is creamy. Add the sugar, egg yolks, milk, and wheatflour. Beat a little more. Add the powdered yeast. Line a rectangular mold, 16 x 11 inches/ 41 x 28cm, with buttered greaseproof paper. Spread the mixture on top of the paper.

Prepare the filling: beat the egg whites until stiff. Add the sugar and beat until a fine meringue is formed. Spread on to the pastry base. Chop half the Brazil nuts into thin slices. Spread over the meringue. Place in a preheated moderate oven (350 °F/180 °C) for 30 minutes or until the meringue is golden brown. Remove from the oven and leave in the mold until the next day.

Turn out the pie and remove the paper. Cut in half widthways. Spread one half with the whipped cream and place the other half on top. Cover with the remainder of the cream. Decorate with the rest of the nuts.

Serves 20

# The perfect couple

6 eggs, separated

6 heaped tbsp/100g sugar

2 cups/250g potato flour

1 tsp/5ml powdered yeast

Butter for greasing

Wheatflour for sprinkling


For the filling:

2 pints/1 l milk

1 cup/250g sugar

6 egg yolks, lightly beaten

2 tbsp/30g cornflour

1 tsp/5ml vanilla essence

Sugar


Beat the egg whites until stiff. Add the egg yolks and beat again until mixed. Add the sugar and beat again. Fold in the potato flour and the yeast.

Grease a baking tray with butter and sprinkle with wheatflour. Place teaspoonsful of the mixture on the tray, leaving a space between. Place in a preheated moderate oven (350 °F/180 °C) until they are golden brown at the base. Remove the tray from the oven immediately and leave to cool.

Prepare the filling: boil the milk with the sugar until it is reduced by half. Add the egg yolks and mix. Strain the filling through a sieve. Add the cornflour and return to the heat until the mixture thickens. Add the vanilla, remove from the heat and leave to cool. Sandwich pairs of biscuits together with the filling. Roll in the sugar.

Makes: 150 perfect pairs

# Bonnes bouches

2 cups/500g sugar

1 cup/250ml water

2 tbsp/30g butter

3 tbsp/75g Parmesan cheese, grated

6 eggs, lightly beaten

3 heaped tbsp/50g sieved wheatflour

Butter for greasing


Mix the sugar with the water and bring to a boil, simmer until it forms a thick syrup the consistency of honey. Leave to cool. Add the butter and cheese, eggs and wheatflour. Mix with a wooden spoon. Place the mixture in 2¾-inch/7cm patty tins greased with butter. Bake in a preheated oven (425 °F/220 °C) until golden brown. Remove from the oven and turn out while hot, after running a knife round the edge of each.

Makes: 20

# "Mother Benedict's" muffins

1 cup/250g butter at room temperature

1 cup/250g sugar

6 egg yolks

2 egg whites, beaten until stiff

1 tsp/5g grated lemon peel

3 cups/375g fine grind rice flour

2 tbsp/30g grated Parmesan cheese

Beat the butter, sugar, and egg yolks until pale and creamy. Add the beaten egg whites, lemon peel, rice flour, and grated cheese. Mix well. Divide the mixture among 25 x 2¾-inch/7cm patty tins lined with paper cake cases. Bake in a preheated moderate oven (350 °F/180 °C) until they are golden brown.

Makes: 25 muffins

# Coconut kisses

2 cups/500g sugar

1 cup/250ml milk

1 tbsp/15g butter

2 cups/250g fresh coconut, grated

2 egg yolks, lightly beaten

1 cup/250ml orange juice

½ tbsp/8g grated orange peel

1 tsp/5g grated lemon peel

1 tsp/5ml vanilla essence

Crystallized sugar

Cloves for decoration

In a saucepan mix together the sugar, milk, and butter and bring to a boil, stirring continuously, for about 15 minutes. Remove from the heat, add the coconut, egg yolks, orange juice, and orange and lemon peel. Return to the heat, stirring continuously. When the mixture comes away from the base of the pan, remove from the heat. Add the vanilla essence. Leave to cool. Roll into small balls between the palms of your hands, moistened with water to prevent the mixture sticking. Roll in the sugar. Insert a clove into the top of each one.

Makes: 60 coconut kisses

# Nut brittle

1 cup/250ml corn syrup

2 cups/500g sugar

3 cups/500g raw unsalted peanuts

4 tbsp/60ml water

2 tsp/10g baking soda

Butter for greasing

Mix all the ingredients together, apart from the baking soda, in a saucepan. Heat until the peanuts begin to break up. Leave to simmer over a low heat for a further 3 minutes. Add the baking soda. Mix well, remove from the heat and beat with a wooden spoon for 30 seconds. With a knife or metal spatula spread the mixture over a marble surface greased with butter. Cool for 5 minutes. With a knife mark in diamond shapes.
When it is lukewarm, break up the brittle along the markings, with the help of a small hammer.

Makes: 30 pieces of brittle

6 cups/1kg green figs

½ tbsp/8g baking soda

3 cups/750ml water

4 cups/1kg crystallized sugar

1 stick cinnamon

1 clove

Wash the figs. Place them in a large pan with enough
water to cover and bring to the boil. Add the baking
soda. Cook for a further 8 minutes and remove from the
heat. Cover and leave to stand overnight.

The next day, scrape the figs carefully with a knife. Make
two small longitudinal cuts in the form of a cross in each
fig and prick them with a toothpick to let out all the milk.
Put the figs in a container with fresh water and leave for
two days, changing the water several times.

Bring the water and crystallized sugar to a boil and
continue boiling until a thin syrup is obtained. Drain the
figs and place them in the syrup. Cook over a low heat
for 30 minutes. Remove from the heat, cover and reserve
until the next day.

Return the pan to a low heat. Add the cinnamon and the
clove and cook until the figs are soft and transparent and
the syrup thick. Remove from the heat and leave to cool.

Serves 8

# Fig compote

30 starfruit

4 cups/1kg sugar

Wash and drain the starfruit. Slice off the ribs and cut off the two ends. Cut in slices using a sharp knife, take out the cores and seeds.

In a large pan place alternate layers of fruit and sugar. Bring to a boil over a low heat, without stirring, until the fruit is soft. Remove the pan from the heat. Take out one ladleful of syrup. Bring to a boil separately until it is golden. Pour this syrup over the fruit. Leave to cool.

Serves 15

# Starfruit in syrup

# Grandmother's fudge

2 pints/1 l milk
4 cups/1kg sugar

In a large saucepan, mix the milk and the sugar. Cook, stirring continuously with a wooden spoon, until it reaches the soft ball stage. To test, take a little of the mixture and place in a small bowl of cold water. It should form a small malleable ball when rubbed between the fingers. Remove from the heat and beat with a wooden spoon until it begins to lose its shine. Spread quickly over an oiled marble surface with a knife or metal spatula. When it is lukewarm cut into diamond shapes.

Serves 8

# Pumpkin compote with coconut

4 cups/1kg ripe pumpkin, peeled
4 cups/1kg sugar
1 large coconut, grated
3 cloves

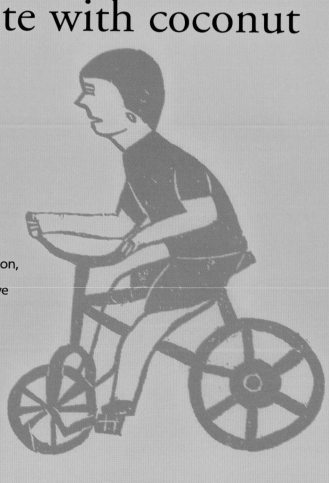

Cook the pumpkin in water until soft. Drain off the water. Mash with a fork. Add the sugar, coconut, and cloves. Cook, stirring continuously with a wooden spoon, until it comes away from the bottom of the pan. Leave to cool.

Serves 8

12 grapefruit

4 small juicing oranges

4 large lemons

7 pints/3 l water

4 cups/1kg sugar

Cloves

2 cinnamon sticks

Peel the grapefruit, oranges, and lemons. Take out the seeds. Cut in thin slices. Cook with the water, sugar, cloves, and cinnamon, leaving the pan uncovered. Stir from time to time. Cook over a low heat for 1 hour or until the oranges are soft. Turn off the heat and leave them to cool.

Serves 12

# Oranges

in syrup

2 or 3 very green papayas

Crystallized sugar

4 cloves

With a sharp knife, score the papaya from top to bottom to let out all the juice. Leave to stand for 2 hours. Wash the papaya well, drain, peel and cut into regular pieces, removing all the seeds. Wash again. Place the fruit in a pan. Cover with water and bring to a boil. Drain. Place the fruit in an earthenware dish, cover with tepid water and leave to stand for 4 hours. Drain.

Weigh the papaya and use the same quantity of sugar. Make a thin syrup with water and sugar. Add the cloves and the papaya. Cook over a low heat until the fruit is very soft. Remove from the heat and leave to stand overnight in its own syrup.

Heat again until the pieces of papaya are transparent and the syrup thick. Do not stir. Remove from the heat and leave to cool.

Serves 8

# Papaya in

syrup

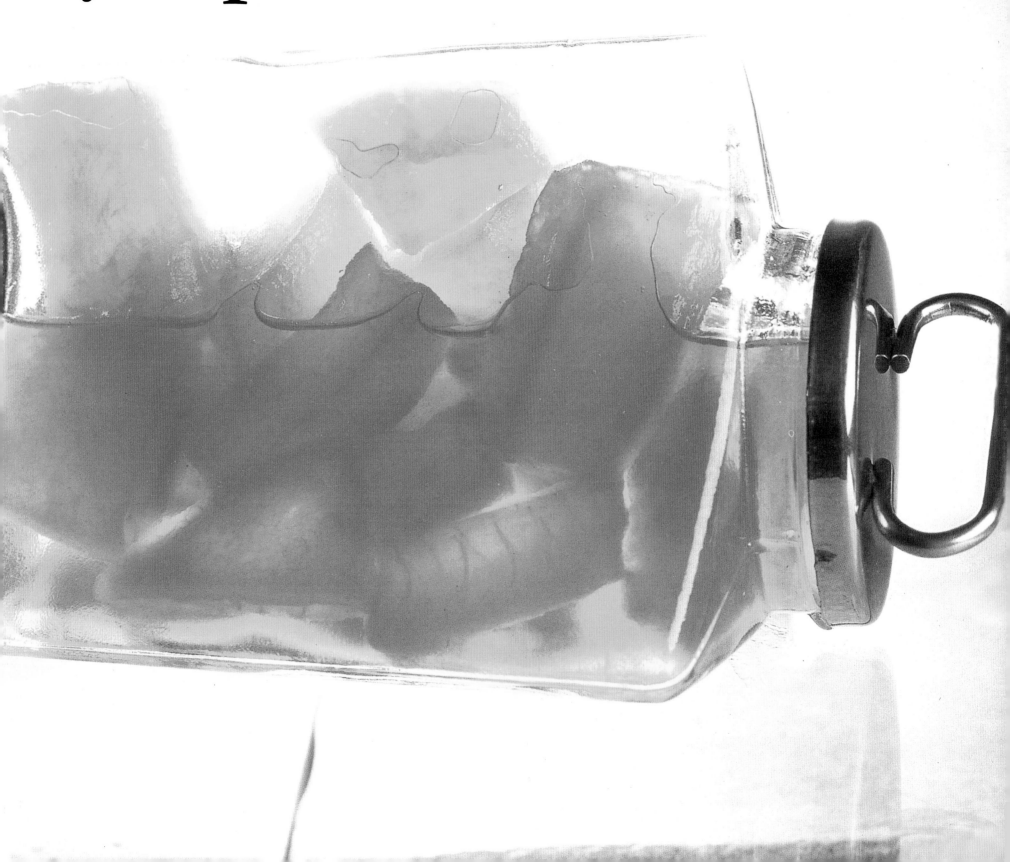

# Pães e biscoitos

# Corn rolls

2 tablets yeast

½ cup/125ml warm milk

1 cup/125g cornmeal

2 cups/500ml water

Pinch of salt

½ cup/125ml oil

1 egg, beaten

4 cups/500g wheatflour

Butter for greasing

Wheatflour for sprinkling

Dissolve the yeast in the milk. Cook the cornmeal, water, and salt, stirring continuously, so that it does not get lumpy. When it boils, reduce the heat and continue stirring until the dough comes away from the bottom of the pan. Remove from the heat and leave to cool. Add the oil, egg, and yeast and mix well. Finally add the wheatflour. Mix. Knead the dough on a floured surface for 10 minutes. Cover and leave to rise for 1 hour. Form into rolls. Place on a greased and floured baking tray, cover again and leave to rise for a further hour. Bake in a preheated hot oven (425 °F/220 °C) for about 45 minutes or until they are golden brown at the base.

Makes: 40 rolls

# Cornmeal scones

3 cups/750ml milk

3 cups/750ml water

6 tbsp/90g sugar

3 tbsp/45g butter or margarine

3 cups/375g cornmeal

Pinch of salt

6 eggs, beaten

Butter for greasing

Wheatflour for sprinkling

In a saucepan boil up the milk, water, sugar, butter or margarine, cornmeal, and salt, stirring continuously with a wooden spoon. When the mixture begins to boil, stir rapidly until it comes away from the pan. Leave to cool and add the beaten eggs, mixing well. Shape into rounds about 2½-inches/6cm in diameter. Place them on a greased and floured baking tray and bake in a preheated hot oven (425 °F/220 °C) for 15 minutes or until they are brown at the base.

Makes: 30 scones

½ cup/125g butter at room temperature

1 cup/250g sugar

2 eggs

2 cups/250g sieved wheatflour

3 tsp/15g powdered yeast

1 tsp/5g salt

1 tbsp/15ml lemon juice

1 cup/150g Brazil nuts, finely chopped

1 cup/200g plantain (cooking bananas), mashed

Butter or margarine for greasing

Wheatflour for sprinkling

Beat the butter with the sugar to form a smooth cream.
Add the eggs and beat a little more. Add the wheatflour,
yeast, salt, and lemon juice. Beat just enough to mix. Add
the Brazil nuts and the bananas. Beat a little more. Fill
into a greased and floured loaf tin (5½ x 10 x 3-inch/
14 x 25 x 7cm). Bake in a preheated moderate oven
(350 °F/180 °C) for about 40 minutes or until golden brown.

Serves 10

# Banana bread

# Yam buns

1 tablet yeast

1 cup/250ml warm milk

½ cup/125g sugar

2 eggs

1 tbsp/15g butter at room temperature

1 tbsp/15g lard at room temperature

1 level tbsp/15g salt

1 medium yam, peeled and grated

6 cups/750g wheatflour

Butter for greasing

Wheatflour for sprinkling

Dissolve the yeast in the warm milk. Add the sugar, eggs, butter, lard, salt, and yam. Mix well. Add enough wheatflour to obtain a dough which does not stick to the hands. Knead a little and leave to rise for 1 hour. Shape rounds 2 inches/5cm in diameter. Place on a buttered and floured baking tray and bake in a preheated hot oven (425 °F/220 °C) for 15 to 20 minutes or until golden brown at the base.

Note: the quantity of wheatflour will vary depending on the size of the yam.

Makes: 35 buns

# Bread filled with cheese

3 cups/375g wheatflour

1 tbsp/15g powdered yeast

Pinch of salt

2 tbsp/50g grated Parmesan cheese

½ cup/125g butter at room temperature

Milk

Wheatflour for sprinkling

Butter for greasing

1 egg, beaten, for coating

For the filling:
Fresh mild cheese, finely chopped

In a bowl mix the sieved wheatflour and yeast together. Add the salt, Parmesan cheese, and butter. Mix with a fork, gradually adding the milk to obtain a dough which does not stick to the fingers. Place the dough on a floured surface and press down lightly. Take small portions of the dough and open them out in the hand (the dough should not be too thick). Fill the rolls with the cheese, seal and shape into small balls. Place the rolls on a greased baking tray. Brush with the beaten egg. Bake in a preheated hot oven (425 °F/220 °C) for 15 to 20 minutes or until golden brown at the base. Serve hot.

Makes: 20 rolls

# Oat cookies

1 cup/125g oats

1 cup/250g sugar

1 cup/125g wheatflour

1 large or 2 small eggs

1 tbsp/15g butter at room temperature

1 tsp/5g powdered yeast

Margarine for greasing

In a bowl mix the oats, sugar, and wheatflour. Add the egg, butter, and yeast. Mix all the ingredients together. Make small balls just under 1 inch (2cm) in diameter. Place them on a greased baking tray leaving a space in between. Press down using a lightly floured fork. Bake in a preheated hot oven (425 °F/220 °C) for 15 minutes or until golden brown at the base. Remove the cookies from the tray and leave to cool.

Makes: 60 cookies

# Arrowroot biscuits

8 cups/1kg arrowroot

6 cups/1.5kg sugar

3 tsp/15g powdered yeast

1 cup/250g butter at room temperature

6 eggs, separated

1½ cups/200g wheatflour

Butter for greasing

Mix the arrowroot, sugar, and yeast. Make a well in the centre and add the butter and the egg yolks. Knead the mixture well with the hands.
Beat the egg whites until stiff. Add to the dough. Add the wheatflour and continue kneading with the hands.
Roll into small balls just under 1 inch (2cm) in diameter. Butter a baking tray. Place the biscuits on it, leaving a space between. Flatten with the hands.
Bake in a preheated moderate oven (350 °F/ 180 °C) for 20 minutes or until golden brown at the base. Remove from the baking tray and leave to cool.

Makes: 150 biscuits

# St. Anthony's biscuits

4 cups/500g sieved wheatflour

1 cup/250g sugar

½ cup/125g butter at room temperature

½ cup/125ml beer

Wheatflour for sprinkling

Butter or margarine for greasing

1 egg white for basting

Crystallized sugar for sprinkling

Mix the flour, sugar, butter, and beer first with a wooden spoon and then with the hands until the dough is smooth.
On a floured surface carefully roll out the dough. Cut into 2-inch/5cm rounds with a pastry cutter or a glass. Butter a baking tray. Place the biscuits on it, leaving a space between them. Brush with the egg white and sprinkle with the sugar.
Bake in a preheated moderate oven (350° F/180° C) for about 15 minutes or until golden brown at the base. Remove the biscuits from the tray and leave to cool.

Makes: 80 biscuits

# Cream cookies

2 cups/500ml cream

2 cups/250g sweet manioc flour

3 cups/375g wheatflour

2 eggs

2 tbsp/30g sugar

Pinch of salt

Pinch of ground cinnamon

Butter or margarine for greasing

Mix all the ingredients together to form a smooth dough. Roll into small sausages, just over 1 inch/3cm long. Place the cookies on a buttered baking tray, leaving a space between. Flatten them with a lightly floured fork. Bake in a preheated hot oven (425 °F/ 220 °C) for about 15 minutes or until they have risen and are slightly brown. Remove from the baking tray and serve hot.

Makes: 80 cookies

3 cups/375g wheatflour

1 tbsp/15g powdered yeast

1 cup/250g sugar

1 cup/100g butter or margarine at room temperature

2 eggs

½ tsp/3g grated nutmeg

3 tbsp/45ml milk

Wheatflour for sprinkling

Oil for frying

Sugar and cinnamon for rolling

Sieve the flour and yeast together in a bowl. Add the sugar. Make a well in the centre and add the butter or margarine, the eggs, and the nutmeg. Gradually add the milk, mixing with a fork. Place the dough on a floured surface. Knead to form a smooth dough. Roll out to a thickness of ½ inch/1cm. Cut into rounds 2¼-inches/6cm in diameter, using a glass or a pastry cutter. Make a ¾-inch/2cm hole in the middle, to form rings. Deep fry in moderately hot oil until golden brown. Drain the donuts on kitchen paper. If to your taste, roll in sugar and/or cinnamon.

Makes: 35 donuts

# St. John's donuts